Pyotr Ilyich
TCHAIKOVSKY

ROMEO & JULIET
OVERTURE-FANTASY
TH 42
(1880 revsion)
Edited by
Clark McAlister

Study Score
Partitur

SERENISSIMA MUSIC, INC.

ORCHESTRA

2 Flutes

Piccolo

2 Oboes

English horn

2 Clarinets in A

2 Bassoons

4 Horns in F

2 Trumpets in C

3 Trombones

Tuba

Timpani

Percussion
(Bass Drum, Cymbals)

Harp

Violin I

Violin II

Viola

Violoncello

Bass

Duration: ca.20 minutes

First performance: March 16, 1870 in Moscow (original version)
Russian Musical Society, Nikolay Rubinstein, conductor
March 1, 1886 in Tbilisi (revised version)
Russian Musical Society of Tiflis
Mikhail Ippolitov-Ivanov, conductor

© Copyright 2014 Clark McAlister.
All rights reserved.

This study score is a reissue – in reduced format – of the large conductor's score. originally issued by the now-defunct E.F. Kalmus as A2181 under the pseudonym Howard K. Wolf. Serenissima Music is proud to be the exclusive publisher of Dr. McAlister's many editions and orchestrations. The large score and orchestral partsare available from Serenissima Music, Inc.

to Mily Balakirev

ROMEO AND JULIET

Overture-Fantasy
(Third Version, 1880)

P. I. TCHAIKOVSKY
Performing Edition by Clark McAlister

---

* The crescendo instructions do not appear in the MS.

Copyright ©2014 Clark McAlister.
20541

* Flutes, Oboes, mm. 213-215: This phrase is slurred thus in the MS:
but compare with mm. 235-237, which are played at a similar dynamic level.

Similarly, at mm. 219-221 Flutes and Oboes are slurred thus in the MS:
but compare with mm. 395-397, which are played at a higher dynamic level.

24

41

49

58

www.ingramcontent.com/pod-product-compliance
Lightning Source LLC
Chambersburg PA
CBHW081349040426
42450CB00015B/3365